GEORGE STEPHENSON

A Life From Beginning to End

Copyright © 2017 by Hourly History.

Table of Contents

Introduction

George Stephenson has many claims to fame associated with his name. Some think he invented the railways. Some believe he invented the steam engine. He did neither. George Stephenson was an engineer without parallel in the first half of the nineteenth century. He was passionate about machinery and became even more passionate about the idea of a locomotive steam engine. He made it his mission to bring about a railway system in which steam locomotives were the motive power.

He wasn't the first to have this ambition, but he was the first to make it a reality. Rails were invented by someone else, but Stephenson brought about a nationwide network of rails and was the first to do it. Steam locomotion was created by someone else, yet Stephenson built the finest locomotives in the world at a time when all other engineers had given up on the idea as impossible.

George Stephenson rose from humble origins to set in motion a transformation of his society that would leave his country a world superpower. He achieved this through a genius for machinery and engineering and a single-minded determination to succeed. To appreciate his achievements, it is necessary to first look at his origins.

Chapter One

A Childhood in Coal

"His favourite amusement at this early age was erecting clay engines with his chosen playmate. The boys found clay for their engines in the adjoining bog, and the hemlocks which grew about supplied them with imaginary steam-pipes. They even proceeded to make a miniature winding engine."

—Samule Smiles

George Stephenson was born on June 9, 1781, in the village of Wylam, near Newcastle. From birth, his world was coal and coal mining. His father Robert, a fireman, was responsible for stoking the static steam engines that pumped water out of mine shafts. Stephenson's first home was situated next to the wooden rails of the Wylam Mine's railway system, built to carry ore from the mine to the coast. Almost everyone in the village and many others in the surrounding area would have worked for, had their homes from, or be in some way associated with the coal mines.

Stephenson was born into an age when coal was in high demand. The industrial revolution consumed the fossil fuel voraciously following the inventions of Thomas Newcomen (inventor of the first practical steam engine in

1712) and the subsequent improvements to Newcomen's engines being made by the ingenious Scot, James Watt. Steam power could improve the efficiency and therefore production of mines. It was also the essential fuel of the industrial revolution all over the country. As a result, a flood of coal ships left the Tyne for London and elsewhere.

Mine workers were amongst the poorest of the working classes. While their labor was in high demand, they were also easily replaced as workers flooded into the once rural communities to find work in the pits. Colliery owners were at the summit of a new feudal system. They owned the land, controlled the availability of employment and even provided the housing in which their workforce lived. Workers could not organize or protest for fear of dismissal. Such was their dependence on the mines that when a pit was worked out, and subsequently closed, the workers would have to move to the next one. Often they followed the same owner, as he bought a new mine to replace the old. This is the grim world into which George Stephenson was born and grew up.

Stephenson's father Robert and his wife Mabel were illiterate, and so was George until his late teens. He was one of six children consisting of two girls and four boys. None were sent to school, as their parents would not have been able to afford it. As was common in in the late eighteenth century, George went to work early in his childhood. His very first job was keeping the neighbor's cows off the mine wagonway. Then, by the age of ten, he had followed his father's footsteps into the mine.

From 1791 to 1795, Stephenson worked in a variety of small jobs at Wylam Mine; driving the horses which pulled the mine carts along the rails for tuppence a day, and picking stones and other unwanted materials out of the coal for sixpence a day. Eventually, at the age of 14, in 1795, George was working alongside his father as an assistant fireman, earning the grand total of a shilling per day. This was the first step in Stephenson's journey of becoming a highly paid skilled worker.

In the late eighteenth century, primitive static steam engines were becoming a common sight up and down the countryside. The steam pumping machine which Robert Stephenson and his son kept stoked had been invented by Thomas Newcombe. It was used to pump water from the mine and open up new seams. A steam-powered winding machine was also used to carry miners to and from the coal face in a cage. Skilled engineers were in charge of those machines, having received the education to be able to maintain them. Stephenson had no education but approached the gaining of knowledge in a much more practical way. To understand the machine he was operating, Stephenson began to dismantle it after the pit had closed, then re-assembling it again. This hands-on learning would be characteristic of George Stephenson throughout his life. His expertise with steam engines was arrived at through trial and error experimentation rather than an in-depth knowledge of the theories behind the machines' operation.

George had always been fascinated by the steam engines used in the colliery. At a young age, he had made models of the pit's various engines out of clay, and once he had received his first job on the great engines, he would remain close to them throughout his life. He would also have been aware, having spent his life around the pits, that it was only through the invaluable machinery that a decent living could be made.

His rise through the pit's pecking order of jobs was rapid and this in itself was unusual for one of such humble origins. It demonstrates his natural affinity for engineering as well as his determination to succeed, despite his lack of education. For his peers, there would have been no opportunity for the professional advancement which George Stephenson achieved from 1791 to 1798, when at the age of 17 he found himself plugman at the Newburn colliery overseeing his father. Robert Stephenson had spent his life in the mines and risen no further than fireman; his son overtook him in just seven years.

But George displayed no contentment at his achievement, nor did his fascination with steam engines end with the steam pump. He worked at understanding all of the machines used in the pits and was called upon regularly to repair them when they broke down. One of the more challenging and demanding jobs at the collieries' machines was operating the winding engine. It was regarded as a more important job than plugman because it was this that allowed the miners to be moved rapidly into and out of the pit.

In the Black Callerton colliery in 1801, at the age of 20, George persuaded the mine's viewer, the general manager, to let him try to operate the winding machine. He did so well he was given the job of brakeman. But now Stephenson hit a roadblock. He was earning £1 a week as an unskilled mechanic. The definition of skilled was to be able to read and write. While he remained illiterate, George would rise no higher, and he was fully aware of this. Some would have been content with a responsible position far above any of their peers, and a wage almost double what their father earned. But Stephenson could not accept that he had reached a plateau.

He wanted to continue rising and to do so needed an education.

Chapter Two

From Illiterate to Engineer

"I have only one son who I have brought up in my own profession. He is now near 20 years of age. I have had him educated in the first Schools and is now at College in Edinburgh. I have found a great want of education myself but fortune has made amends for that want."

—George Stephenson, in a letter talking about his son Robert

George Stephenson was throughout his life a practical man. He desired to learn to read and write because it would aid his advancement and because it was a far more efficient way of learning about the machines he loved. It was around 1799, at the age of 18, that Stephenson met a young viewer named Nicholas Wood. This man would remain a friend and champion of Stephenson for many years. Wood had earned his position following an education in which he had qualified as an engineer. Stephenson would have realized the difference between the two of them immediately. Wood could design and build the engines which Stephenson was only able to run and maintain.

So, Stephenson set about attending night classes in the village of Walbottle in 1799. He received additional coaching from a local farmer, and within three years he understood the basics of reading and writing. Arithmetic seems to have come easier to Stephenson because for years after he would get other people to read aloud and write for him. There are many letters in existence dictated by George Stephenson, but it is very rare to find any in his own handwriting.

It was during this period, at the age of 21, that Stephenson made his first marriage proposal. The object of his affections was Elizabeth Hindmarsh, daughter of a wealthy farmer. Unfortunately, her family disapproved of her marrying an anonymous pitman with no prospects that they could recognize, despite Stephenson's ambitions. They refused the match. While George appears to have moved on quickly to another girl, Elizabeth refused to marry anyone else. The two would meet again and finally have their wedding almost 20 years later.

But for now, Stephenson proposed next to Ann Henderson, a servant at the farm in which he had his lodgings. He was refused and asked again, this time of her older sister Frances, known as Fanny. She accepted, and the two were wed on November 28, 1802. The couple moved to Willington Quay, where Stephenson took a position as brakeman on a newly installed winding machine. Their only son, Robert Stephenson, was born almost a year after the ceremony, on October 16, 1803.

Compared to the circumstances Stephenson had grown up in, Robert would have found himself in a relatively comfortable home. It was customary for multiple families to share the colliery cottages.

Stephenson had grown up in a cottage in which eight families had shared two rooms. In his own married home, Stephenson was able to secure three rooms for himself, Fanny and Robert alone. This demonstrates his relatively high income, for an uneducated working man. As well as the wage he earned from the pit, Stephenson supplemented his income making shoes and mending clocks.

This gives an insight into the moral character of the young Stephenson. It was commonplace in mining communities for men to forget the harshness of their work, the poor living conditions, and wages by indulging in gambling and drink come payday. In fact, communities like Wylam, Willington Quay, and others would have been riotous on the fortnightly payday. Stephenson resisted this urge. He can be seen, in his early twenties, working hard at both his job and is education, being responsible with his money, and doting on his infant son. He would retain his relentless work ethic throughout his life.

The move to Willington Quay appears to have been motivated by Stephenson's interest in a new kind of static steam engine. It was being used to pull mine carts uphill and had been invented by Robert Hawthorn who had recommended Stephenson for the post of brakeman on the machine. This innovation was designed to make the process of getting ore to market faster and therefore make the mine more profitable. It removed the need for horses to pull the carts uphill, cutting the costs of keeping the animals.

In 1804, at the age of 23, Stephenson moved his family to the village of Killingworth, where he was employed as a brakeman. Fanny gave birth to a daughter there who, sadly, died at just three weeks old. The family tragedy did not end there, and one year later, Fanny also died, of consumption (tuberculosis). At this point, Stephenson appears to have left his two-year-old son in the care of a neighbor and headed for Scotland. Little is known about his motivation for this or what he did while he was away. He returned after just a few months, £28 richer, and took up his old cottage once more. His sister Eleanor moved in to look after young Robert.

It was at this time that the owner of the Wylam colliery, where Stephenson had begun his career, invested in a locomotive steam engine designed by Richard Trevithick, the famed Cornish engineer. The engine was being built for him in a Gateshead workshop. At the time this would have been state of the art technology, and Stephenson would certainly have been aware of it. The engine was never put into service, but Stephenson would in just a few years turn to locomotive technology himself. But for the moment, it seemed his priority was his family and his job as a brakeman.

Robert Stephenson Senior had suffered an accident while George was away, losing his job and running up debts. George used his savings to settle his father's debts and then moved both parents to Killingworth where he continued to support them until their deaths. Meanwhile, George continued to work as a brakeman at the Killingworth pit.

It may be that following the death of his daughter and wife Stephenson had experienced a further blow, the loss of his brakeman job at Killingworth. This would explain his departure from Tyneside on foot, supposedly for Scotland. Robert Hawthorne, who had been his patron, may have quarreled with Stephenson and subsequently dismissed him. Stephenson's biographers note that, particularly as a young man, he was loathed to acknowledge any who may have aided in his success. George was the epitome of the self-made man and liked it to be known that he had accomplished all by himself. This was another trait he would retain throughout his life, and it would prove a trait which others found disagreeable.

Whatever the reason for this absence it does not appear to have been the result of any lack of care for his family. His actions in supporting his parents show that he took his responsibilities as a successful son very seriously. His devotion to his son's education in the coming years would further support this view. For now, George Stephenson was a 25-year-old with a reputation as a brilliant engineer, if so far still technically unskilled. He was a family man, and over the next few years, this would be demonstrated by the keen interest he took in Robert's education.

Chapter Three

The Self-Made Man

"Engineers for the most part began as simple workmen, skillful and ambitious but usually illiterate or self-taught. They were either millwrights like Bramah, mechanics like Murdoch and George Stephenson, or smiths like Newcomen."

—John Desmond Bernal

In 1811, when George Stephenson was 30 years old, a new mine at Killingworth received a Newcomen pumping machine. The engine gave constant trouble for 12 months. Stephenson proclaimed that he could fix it and was offered the chance by a Mr. Dodds, the head viewer. Stephenson specified that he would only work with men of his choice. It is likely that the engineers who had tried to get the machine working for a year would have been less than cooperative with the upstart brakeman who insisted on telling them their jobs. There certainly appears to have been a streak of arrogance in George Stephenson's attitude towards his work. He had earned himself his first brakeman job by his boasting that he could do it, despite being a lowly fireman at the time.

But his boasts were well-founded then, as now. In three days the machine was working, and Stephenson earned a promotion. He became the colliery engine-wright and was subsequently responsible for all the mine's machinery. He received £100 per year for this work. In comparison, at 12 shillings per week, his father would have made £30 a year as a fireman. But it didn't stop there; Stephenson's abilities were much more in demand. His skills had come to the attention of a group of wealthy mine owners, the Grand Alliance, and he started building and maintaining engines for them. He was also allowed to do freelance work for other collieries. It is a testament to how valued Stephenson was at Killingworth that this was permitted.

Robert Stephenson was by now attending school. He graduated from a village school at Long Benton to a prestigious Newcastle academy and then the Literary and Philosophical Society of Newcastle. But it wasn't just for his own career that he was being educated; as Robert learned, so did George. Robert would ride home from the Academy of Doctor Bruce in Newcastle with books which he would read aloud to his father; the two then debated the theories contained within. Eventually, George would accompany his son into the Literary and Philosophical Society to study together. He was reluctant to do so at first because of his humble origins. He still had a thick, rural Northumbrian accent which some of the more elevated members of Newcastle society found almost unintelligible. It seems this was something Stephenson was self-conscious about; he was aware of the class divisions, the class he came from and which Robert at least had transcended.

George Stephenson had already demonstrated a difficulty in learning from other adults. The self-made man seemed incapable of acknowledging the help of any other man in his own betterment. He disliked being told something he didn't know if it came from a man who had received the advantages which Stephenson hadn't. He had worked his way through the professional strata of the mines and would have continually seen men senior to himself, with academic pedigrees, while his learning had to come through trial and error. But when the new knowledge came from his educated son things seemed different. As one learned, so did the other.

And as Robert was nearing the end of his education, an event occurred which illustrates the attitudes of many towards the self-made man, and serves to illustrate a reason for Stephenson's resentment.

Chapter Four

The Safety Lamp Controversy

"The principles upon which a safety lamp might be constructed I stated to several persons long before Sir Humphrey Davy came into this part of the country."

—George Stephenson

A common problem in coal mining had always been fire and explosions. Any underground mine contained combustible gases and, prior to the invention of the electric light, miners would use naked flames to light lamps while underground. They had no way of knowing if they were in the midst of a pocket of combustible gases and the result was frequent accidents. This was of great concern to mine owners, and in 1815, a group of North East colliery owners wanted to solve the problem, and they turned to an eminent scientific authority.

Sir Humphrey Davy was accounted one of the foremost scientific minds of his generation, and on August 24, 1815, he was invited to inspect the mines of the northeast and devise a solution to the problem. Another man was already at work on the problem, though he lacked the public profile of Davy. That was the engine-wright of the Killingworth colliery, George Stephenson.

Davy published a paper on November 9, 1815, unveiling his safety lamp, which would provide illumination with no risk of starting a fire. He was lauded for this invention, and it was taken up by mines all over the country. One area did not take up use of the Davy lamp, however, the northeast. That was because on December 5, 1815, at the Newcastle Literary and Philosophical Society, George Stephenson unveiled his own design. It was virtually identical to Davy's and was just as effective. The Geordie lamp was taken up in the mines of Tyneside, and a highly public campaign began to win recognition for George Stephenson as its inventor.

This campaign went on in the nation's press for two years and resulted in some highly charged opinions being expressed. Stephenson was accused of stealing the theories of Davy, the great man of science. None in the Davy camp could believe that a pitman from an obscure background with no formal education could have arrived at the same design as Sir Humphrey Davy.

To resolve the matter once and for all, a meeting was held in the Newcastle Assembly Rooms on November 1, 1817. The committee heard detailed evidence relating to the timing of the respective invention's development. Included in this evidence was the testimony of a tinsmith who claimed that Stephenson had provided him with the blueprints of his design for manufacture between October 2 and 7, 1815. This would have been almost a month before Davy unveiled his invention.

The committee found in Stephenson's favor, and he was awarded £1,000 and credited with being the "first to apply in construction" the principle of the safety lamp. The ordeal elevated Stephenson's name to public attention for the first time.

It also serves to demonstrate the method of learning he applied throughout his life; there was plentiful evidence of Stephenson's invention pre-dating Davy's because Stephenson made so many prototypes. He worked on a trial and error basis to reach the solution: a way of lighting the lamp without setting fire to the gases. Davy reached the same conclusion but did so from a good understanding of the chemistry involved. Stephenson did not know about chemistry, but he knew what he saw in his experiments, what worked and what didn't.

It goes some way to explain the resentment Stephenson demonstrated towards men of learning, especially when they were challenging his expertise. Learning by trial and error would be a long and difficult process, it's likely that Stephenson would have had a measure of envy for those whose academic background could lead them to a solution so much more directly. It was, after all, the reason he had so fervently pursued his own education. Stephenson also would have been victim to a great deal of prejudice and discrimination. This was certainly the case with the conflict between himself and Humphrey Davy.

Chapter Five

The Blücher

"The locomotive engine of Mr. Stephenson is superior beyond all comparison to all the other engines I have ever seen. Next to the immortal Watt I consider Stephenson's merit in the invention of this engine."

—William James

George Stephenson is often thought of as being the inventor of the locomotive steam engine. This is far from the case, but he did make the locomotive steam engine a commercial success, thus paving the way for the revolution in transport technology that would transform the world. Without his foresight, the Victorian era of the late nineteenth century would have looked very different.

Richard Trevithick of Cornwall was the first to invent a locomotive steam engine in 1801, though he never solved the problems that meant it could never be commercially viable. His machine used roughly made gears as part of its operation; it would eventually shake itself to pieces. It broke down frequently as a result of the stresses imposed by its mechanisms. His first engine ran on roads, his second, in 1804, ran on rails. Though Trevithick's second locomotive was viable in terms of its ability to pull freight, it was far too heavy for the rails on which it ran, destroying them as it went. This was a problem would plague the early locomotive steam engines, including Stephenson's first creation, the *Blücher*.

The *Blücher* first ran on July 25, 1814, at Killingworth. It was described as having two cylinders, an eight-foot-long boiler, and flanged wheels. It proved capable of pulling thirty tons of freight at four miles an hour. As with his previous learning, Stephenson developed his locomotive engineering by trial and error, and he continually refined the *Blücher* to improve it. He designed a blast pipe to reduce noise and increase boiler pressure, and replaced the gears with connecting rods that drove the wheels. This would become a commonplace arrangement on steam locomotives.

There was a great need for locomotive steam engines driven by the high cost of using horses as motive power. The Napoleonic war had placed high demands on the nation's horse stocks, and the cost of fodder had skyrocketed. An alternative would save an enormous amount of money and decrease the price of coal as a result by making it far easier to bring to market. But most other locomotive engineers appeared to be discouraged by the failures that mounted up around their engines. The problem of the rails was a particular issue. From 1814 to about 1826, no new locomotives were being built across the country—except for those built by George Stephenson.

Stephenson was the only one to tackle both improvements to his engines at the same time as the problem of the weak rails. He entered into a partnership with William Losh, who ran a Newcastle ironworks, to develop a new kind of rail which would withstand the weight of his locomotives. Meanwhile, Stephenson developed 16 locomotives up to 1826, mostly for Killingworth. The Killingworth wagonway was also relaid with the new Losh-Stephenson rails.

Word began to spread during this time. Engineers from across the country, as well as interested parties from across Europe, were visiting Tyneside to see Stephenson's locomotives. In 1819, at Hetton colliery, an entirely new rail line was laid. It used a hybrid system of locomotives, static steam engines, and self-acting planes to provide the motive power.

George Stephenson was 38 years old when the Hetton line was built, and his work was the subject of books and newspaper articles from as far afield as Germany. Just four years earlier, he had been an obscure pitman, whom few could believe had bested the famous Sir Humphrey Davy.

Chapter Six

The Stockton-Darlington Railway

"To tell you the truth although it would put £500 in my pockets to specify my own patent rails, I cannot do so after the experience I have had."

—George Stephenson in a letter to the Stockton-Darlington company board on seeing Birkinshaw's malleable metal rails.

A project was being conceived which would catapult Stephenson to nationwide fame: the first, steam-powered, public railway. This would become one of the projects which Stephenson would be closely associated with and celebrated for, though its beginnings would be fairly modest.

In 1817, a Quaker businessman from Darlington, named Edward Pease, decided to withdraw from his business to devote himself to a worthy cause. To make money from benefiting others was a motive which was approved of by the Quaker faith, and the cause which Pease chose was a horse-drawn railway carrying coal from South Durham mines to the coast. The reason he saw this as a benefit to the public was that those mines were inland, further inland than the Tyneside collieries, and the largest single cost in their operation was the transportation of the ore to the ships which would carry them to London and other markets. Tyneside collieries had an effective monopoly of this trade because of the relative ease with which they could bring their goods to the market.

Pease decided that a railway would reduce the cost of transportation, therefore reducing the cost of the coal, therefore benefiting local people and the local economy. So, he set about bringing his dream to fruition. In mid-1818 he formed a company named the Stockton-Darlington Railway Company. As this was to be a public railway, an Act of Parliament was required for it to begin operation, and this was obtained on April 19, 1821.

On the same day, Edward Pease received a visit from George Stephenson. By this point in his career, Stephenson was a well-respected colliery engine-wright with a sizeable income in the form of salary, freelance fees, and investments. In 1820, he had taken out a lease on a colliery of his own, Willow Bridge, moving from the status of employee to employer for the first time. He was accompanied by his long-standing friend and colleague Nicholas Wood.

They had attempted to see Leonard Railsback, a Stockton solicitor who was one of the Stockton-Darlington Railway Company's subscribers. Railsback had not been at home, and the pair had walked to Darlington where Stephenson was able to present himself and his letters of recommendation to Pease. The next day, Pease wrote to Stephenson formally asking him to survey the route of the Stockton-Darlington railway. Stephenson accepted the post on April 28, 1821, though he caveated that this would be one of many projects he was currently engaged in, and it would not receive all of his attention. He was officially appointed to survey the route for the railway in July 1821.

At this point, the Stockton-Darlington railway had been incorporated as a horse-drawn railway, and the company seal depicted a wagon being drawn by a team of horses. The company's first surveyor of the route to be taken, George Overton, had concluded that steam locomotives would not be practical. Despite this, Stephenson was confident he would be allowed to run locomotives on the line.

Stephenson completed the survey by January 1822 with the help of a new assistant hired for the job, John Dixon, and his own son, Robert. Later that year, Robert Stephenson was invited to join one William James in a survey of a railway line between Liverpool and Manchester. James had made himself something of an expert on railway matters and had surveyed many possible lines across the country. He and Robert were to become good friends during the course of their work together. This job was to have a profound subsequent impact on both the relationship between father and son and on Stephenson's reputation.

In May 1822, Stephenson was appointed engineer to the Stockton-Darlington railway, among his many other commissions. He had already persuaded the company to use cast iron rails. This would have financially benefited Stephenson because of the patent he and William Losh held on the design, which would have meant royalties paid to them by the company. However, in 1821, an engineer in Morpeth named John Birkinshaw had patented a new method of producing malleable metal rails. Stephenson realized that Birkinshaw's rails were superior to his own and decided that these must be the tracks used.

This demonstrates the integrity which Stephenson possessed. He was recommending what he regarded as the best materials despite his vested interests. He even used this fact to persuade the company to his way of thinking. The rails were more expensive, but Stephenson was forceful when it came to knowing what was best. He won over the company board with the force of his personality and boundless confidence. On this project, Stephenson would be a true pioneer. He would be using materials never tried before, encountering new problems, and devising his solutions to those problems.

One decision was to have an impact on the development of railways across the country and the world: the gauge used for the rails. The gauge was the distance between the rails, and Stephenson decided this should be set at 4 feet, 8.5 inches. There is some question about how Stephenson chose this specific distance to set the gauge of his rails. One theory is that this was the standard cart width used by the Romans, though there is no evidence one way or the other. It was the gauge Stephenson had used at Killingworth, and it would be the gauge adopted by the Liverpool-Manchester line. It would come to be known as the "standard gauge" and, by a later Act of Parliament, was the standard to which all other railways would be built.

Stephenson approached the construction of the Stockton-Darlington line with a meticulous eye for detail, taking all major decisions himself, despite his workload. He was to delegate far more on the next major line he constructed, and this would prove to his great detriment.

The first rail was ceremonially laid on May 23, 1822, at Stockton. From his letters, Stephenson was determined that the railway would carry steam locomotives, but in construction, at this stage, he was forced to build for horses. Sleepers needed to be laid along the direction of travel, rather than transversely, to allow for horses walking in between the rails. Stephenson traveled the length and breadth of the country for this aspect of the project alone; going to London to inspect oak blocks, then to Durham to see locally quarried stone, then to South Wales to look at iron.

This was partly due to Stephenson's limitless confidence in his abilities and partly due to the fact that there was no-one else in the country doing what he was doing. Railways were in their infancy in the 1820s, and those that existed were not exclusively steam powered. But for the Stockton-Darlington, Stephenson had decided it would be steam and was taking the company along with him. His locomotives were the best in the country, in fact, the only ones in the country, and therefore the railway would have them.

While the line was being constructed, an amendment was required to the original Act of Parliament which had created the line. This amendment was to allow for the use of locomotives. Stephenson had won over Pease by showing him the Killingworth and Hetton railways, and subsequently, the board had also been persuaded. It was Stephenson's first experience of lobbying. His trenchant views on the landed gentry came to the fore in this process. Lord Shaftesbury, an extremely influential parliamentarian, had not heard of a locomotive. This is understandable considering the relative newness of the technology. In a letter, Stephenson described him as a "fool" and "a spoilt child." This is evidence of a trait in Stephenson's nature that would cause him problems later. He always believed that he knew best and had a difficult time limiting himself to another's intellect when he regarded it as inferior to his own. It made him overconfident and this would cause problems in the near future.

But not at this point. The amended Act was passed on May 23, 1823, and the Stockton-Darlington railway was officially locomotive driven. The following month, Stephenson, Pease, and Michael Longridge formed a locomotive company to begin the manufacture of engines for the Stockton-Darlington line. Longridge was the owner of the ironworks which were making Birkinshaw's patented malleable rails. And Stephenson's son, Robert, was appointed manager of the works.

The new enterprise was sited in Newcastle, and Stephenson and his wife moved house to be nearer to it.

The year 1824 was to prove a busy period for George Stephenson, where he was inundated with work requests. Many were requests to survey new railway lines; there was a growing interest in the concept and the idea of steam locomotion. Enthusiasts such as William James were writing pamphlets on the subject which were being circulated across the country, and a small but influential group of steam fans was persuading many businessmen of the benefits.

At the same time, there was an extremely vocal lobby who opposed steam locomotion. There were a number of hysterical opinions being expressed on the subject of the potential speed of these engines and the detrimental effect of that speed. It was a common fear of the time that any vehicle exceeding ten miles an hour would lead to the deaths of the passengers aboard. Landowners objected to the railways being laid across their lands, while owners of turnpike roads, and canal and river traders protested to protect their vested interests. The country was divided between the vocal, but ignorant, masses and the passionate aficionados like William James and George Stephenson.

Nevertheless, the Stockton-Darlington line received its grand unveiling on September 9, 1825, with great ceremony. One engine, the *Locomotion*, was transported down from Newcastle, and it pulled thirty-three wagons and three hundred passengers along the nine miles from Darlington to Stockton. Many more spectators clambered aboard en route. At Stockton, they picked up wagons of coal and flour as well as more passengers, extending the length of the total train to 400 feet, with a weight of 90 tons. It was an unmitigated success, reaching an unheard of 15 miles an hour on the downhill sections without any harm to its passengers.

Though the Stockton-Darlington line was just a small, regional colliery railway, its importance cannot be understated. It provided a solid demonstration of the correctness of Stephenson's beliefs; people could travel on locomotives at—for those days—high speeds and come to no harm. More importantly, he proved that locomotives had a part to play in the transportation of goods. Freight haulage did not have to be by horse. Any mine, mill, or factory owner in the United Kingdom could read about the use of locomotives on the Stockton-Darlington line and how long it took to transport ore from mine to ship. They could do the math as to how much money they would be saving from such rapid transportation of their goods to market as well as raw materials to their premises.

In the previous decade, George Stephenson had been the only man making steam locomotives in the country. All others had supposedly given up on the idea. To be the only one building them meant he couldn't rely on anyone else to solve the problems that came up, had he been inclined to do so. He was encountering the problems and pitfalls first, and so was the first to solve those problems. His achievement in delivering a working railway in so short a time is made more remarkable when viewed through that lens.

Chapter Seven

The Liverpool-Manchester Failure

"What can be palpably more absurd than the prospect held out of locomotives travelling twice as fast as stagecoaches?"

—The Quarterly Review, March 1825

One of the professional groups who had read about the Stockton-Darlington line and was persuaded by its example was the Liverpool-Manchester Railway Company. The members of the company approached Stephenson with a request to survey a line for them between Liverpool and Manchester on May 19, 1824. The proposed line was intended to accelerate the passage of cotton from Liverpool's docks to Manchester's mills.

From the beginning of the century, the quantity of cotton imported to Liverpool from the United States had increased hugely, the population of the city skyrocketing as a result. At first, all goods had to be shipped by river before a canal was built to allow for goods to be shipped faster. But this was still not fast enough. Merchants in Manchester complained about the weeks of waiting to see their goods moved off the docks. There were huge queues every day at the offices of the canal agents with people waiting to arrange for transportation that way. It became clear that there was far more trade than the waterways could accommodate.

So, William James had been appointed to complete a survey for the line, and Robert Stephenson worked with him on the project. But James was beset by financial problems, he was slow to produce his final survey and was then imprisoned for bankruptcy. The company decided to appoint a new engineer to survey the line for them and chose George Stephenson. This decision caused a gulf between father and son.

It was around this time that Robert Stephenson was preparing to embark on an adventure to explore gold mining, first in Mexico and then in South America. His letters of the time make reference to a warm climate being of benefit to his health. He had, after all, spent years working in coal mines and had a history of poor health from his mother's side. However, this meant being absent from the opening of the Stockton-Darlington railway, where a locomotive built in his works would be undertaking its maiden trip. It was also a significant moment in his father's life.

Another possible reason that has been suggested for Robert's absence is that he had become close friends with William James, who had subsequently lost his position to George Stephenson. James had sorely needed the job of engineer for the company. His profession had been as a land agent, but he appears to have allowed his business to slide while he pursued railway surveys up and down the country. None of this railway work ever became anything solid for him, and meanwhile, his business had gone bankrupt. The Liverpool-Manchester line must have seemed to be his last hope. Even while in prison James clung to his survey notes, refusing to give them up.

Robert Stephenson had become good friends with James and may well have felt that his father was doing the man a disservice. Given the delays James had caused to the Liverpool-Manchester Company, it is understandable that they wanted to part ways, but it could be argued that Stephenson had a moral obligation to his son's friend.

But Stephenson had already demonstrated a willingness to sacrifice relationships on the altar of business. His insistence on using the malleable metal rails for example, at the expense of his and William Losh's patented product. Had it been Stephenson alone who held the interest in the cast iron rails it would seem a selfless act to give up the extra profit in favor of a superior product. But William Losh was not consulted before Stephenson, as engineer of the Stockton-Darlington line, but also his business partner, decided not to use cast iron rails.

It would appear that Robert Stephenson may have felt so aggrieved at his father that he wished to take himself away for a while. Whatever the reason for his overseas trip, it meant he was not assisting his father on the surveying of the Liverpool-Manchester line as he had done for the Stockton-Darlington line. Nor was he present during the subsequent parliamentary debate on the bill to bring the Liverpool-Manchester line into law.

George Stephenson began his survey in 1824. From the outset, the survey of the new line was more difficult than it had been for the Stockton-Darlington, and the vested interests opposed to the railway were more powerful. The private landowners who would need to give their consent were amongst the wealthiest and most influential in the country. Stephenson was no longer working for a little-known Quaker businessman in a small northern county; he was in the powerhouse of the industrial north. Liverpool's port was eclipsing Bristol as Britain's primary west coast harbor while Manchester was the heart of Britain's huge textile industry.

Lords such as Sefton, Derby, and Bradshaw armed their retainers and set them to shoot at trespassing surveyors who tried to set foot on their lands. Local people were marshaled to attack the surveyors wherever they could be found. Stephenson resorted to completing his surveys at night in order to escape hostile attention. He also sent decoy surveyors out to draw the fire of the landowners and their employees. Stephenson recruited Paul Padley to assist him, William James' brother-in-law. Padley had worked with James and Robert Stephenson on the previous survey, so he had a knowledge of the area.

With Padley's support and Stephenson's skill, the challenging survey was completed by the end of 1824. Stephenson rapidly produced a summary including his costs by February 1825. The following month, a parliamentary debate on the Act required to bring the Liverpool-Manchester line into being was begun. Stephenson was called to give evidence in April 1825.

His first project, the Stockton-Darlington line, was five months from completion at this point, but Stephenson must have been feeling confident. He had already had experience of lobbying politicians and had managed it successfully for the Stockton-Darlington project. He was also hugely confident in his engineering skills and the quality of his engines. So far in his career, Stephenson had encountered no real failures, and he was by nature a very self-assured man. The counsel for the Liverpool-Manchester Company, Henry Brougham, cautioned him, however, against displaying too much confidence. For example, when the question turned to that of speed, Stephenson had been on record as stating he believed he could produce engines that could reach 20 miles an hour.

Brougham advised Stephenson to talk only of much lower speeds for fear of losing credibility. But Stephenson, as usual, found it difficult to be modest and even harder to take instruction from an educated man of a higher social class on his own subject of expertise. After all, George Stephenson had never been good at understating his ability.

When questioned by Edward Alderson, Stephenson said the speed on the line would be around four miles an hour. He then added that much more would be possible. This was Stephenson's first mistake. Alderson was able to return, throughout his questioning, to the subject of speed. It must be remembered that for the nation as a whole, the speed of locomotives felt like a genuine safety concern. The Stockton-Darlington line would not prove these fears unfounded for another five months. Accepted theory was that speeds of ten miles an hour or more were injurious to life. Hearing Stephenson admit the line would be capable of traveling faster than a safe speed of eight miles an hour was damning to his cause.

Despite this, Stephenson answered questions put to him on speed and safety with confidence. He did have the example of the Killingworth colliery line to point to as a demonstration of the effectiveness and safety of locomotive engines. But when the questions moved on to the survey itself, his credibility was shattered. Because of the limited time he had to complete the survey and the immense workload which he had at the time, Stephenson had delegated much of the measuring work. During the cause of the debate, many of the figures taken by his team were proven wrong. And where Stephenson had done the work himself, he was worryingly vague about vital information.

He was questioned about the width of the Irwell River to be crossed, and could not answer. Nor could he say what the base level had been which his measurements of the height of the railway line and any bridges relied on. Experts were brought in, such as engineer William Cubitt, to check the figures and they were found to be incorrect throughout the survey. One set of estimates of the height required for a bridge over the Irwell River was actually below the highest flood point of the river. Stephenson was forced to admit that he had not taken the measurements, they had been taken for him.

Stephenson's confidence, it appears, was shattered by this cross-examination. Edward Alderson made his name from his comprehensive assassination of George Stephenson's credibility, and the bill was defeated and subsequently withdrawn. Stephenson had not been able to communicate his knowledge and unquestionable talent effectively. He was a man who had successfully built two colliery railways, Killingworth and Hetton, with a third under construction and not yet proven. But he was not an educated, sophisticated, courtly man used to parliamentary language or the sophistry of courtroom debates. Stephenson still possessed a thick Northumbrian accent that would have been sneered at by the London upper classes.

Had this defeat been entirely based on the reluctance of the upper class elite to accept the knowledge of a working class, self-taught northerner, it would be possible to feel sympathy for Stephenson. But, he had, it seems, overstretched himself, especially since his son's departure abroad. Stephenson's survey was found to be full of errors and assumptions. Neither of these would be considered acceptable in the field which George Stephenson had chosen for himself. An engineer must be precise above all, and the Liverpool-Manchester survey was proven to be anything but exact.

Following the defeat, the board of the Liverpool-Manchester Company dismissed Stephenson and hired another surveyor.

Chapter Eight

The Rocket Takes Over the World

"The rage for railroads is so great that many will be laid in parts that will not pay."

—George Stephenson

Following Stephenson's humiliation and dismissal, the board of the Liverpool-Manchester Railway Company hired two famous Scottish engineers to oversee completion of a new survey: George and John Rennie. Their survey adjusted Stephenson's route slightly and was subsequently passed by Act of Parliament on May 5, 1826. Part of the Act stipulated that locomotives would be used on the line, but it was a small clause designed not to attract attention. The Rennies were too busy to accept the post of chief engineers for the construction of the line but agreed to act in a supervisory capacity. Their compromise, however, was turned down, and the board looked again to George Stephenson.

This time, his contract was tightly bound with conditions, chief of which was that he must give their line his undivided attention. Stephenson never adhered fully to this stipulation as he also had contracts to build lines in

Bolton, Canterbury, and Wales. However, he did relocate his home to Liverpool and brought over his trusted assistants, such as John Dixon, that he had used to build the Stockton-Darlington line.

Stephenson's credibility had risen since the opening of that line, with the locomotive being shown to be capable of carrying goods. It seems to have boosted Stephenson's confidence too. He rapidly dispensed with the services of the engineer appointed to work with him, Charles Vignoles, and now exerted full control over every aspect of the line he was building.

Robert Stephenson was still in America at this time and was asked to return to take over the Newcastle locomotive works. Letters between father and son survive which demonstrate the amicable nature of their relationship. If they did part over the treatment of William James, their separation would seem to have repaired the rift by this point. Robert returned to Newcastle to take up the reins of his locomotive works while his father continued to build the Liverpool-Manchester line.

Stephenson's biggest challenge by far was the infamous Chat Moss bog. His failed survey had been ridiculed in Parliament for his proposal to take the train track through the bog, and when faced with it in practice, it seemed an insurmountable obstacle. Stephenson decided to take the approach of sinking ballast into the bog in order to fill it so that a foundation would be formed, across which the line could be floated. As this work went on, it seemed that the bog must surely be bottomless because however much material Stephenson's navvies put in, it sank and was not seen again. Still, Stephenson's letters state that he was convinced that his plan would work.

By 1828, the board ran out of money and was forced to apply to the government for a loan. The government agreed, but only if the work could be surveyed by an established engineer who could advise them on the progress. The engineer chosen was Thomas Telford, one of the most famous men in the field. Stephenson's reaction was predictable. He ensured he was unavailable when Telford sent an assistant to speak to him. He refused to co-operate and eventually Telford himself had to go out to reason with Stephenson. His findings were that the line would be significantly more expensive than Stephenson was estimating, and that locomotives would not be the best motive power.

Eventually, Stephenson had to sign a contract agreeing to complete the line by 1830, but whether it would have locomotives operating on it was still in question. The company board preferred the idea of using stationary engines and a system of ropes to pull the wagons along. George and Robert Stephenson, however, were convinced that only locomotives would do. The Stockton-Darlington line was open, but rumors were circulating of slow speeds and numerous accidents, and there were still many vocal opponents of locomotives.

A deputation went to Darlington to investigate and decide which motive power would be the most effective. They reported back that fixed steam engines would be the best. Stephenson's response was a 4,000-word essay in which he argued for locomotives. He was persuasive enough that the board sent a second deputation to Darlington. In March 1829, the second evaluation produced the same result as the first. Stationary steam engines were cheaper than locomotives in transporting goods. However, Robert Stephenson argued strongly that his works were planning more effective locomotives which would prove cheaper than the estimated cost of using static engines.

The board was still undecided and subsequently set up a competition to find the best engine in April 1829. The competition would be held at a stretch of completed line at Rainhill later that year. The locomotive which the Stephensons would put into the contest would be called the *Rocket*. Its chief innovation was its multi-tube boiler. To increase the surface area inside the boiler capable of carrying heat, 25 copper tubes were inserted. This was a first in locomotive engineering and would be a feature of steam engines until the end of the steam era. Another feature was the blast pipe, which carried steam from the cylinders back into the chimney and served to maintain the pressure. This was an innovation Stephenson appears to have arrived at years earlier entirely by accident. Nevertheless, it worked.

By the summer of 1829, Stephenson had finally solved the problem of the Chat Moss bog and had completed the impressive Edgehill tunnel beneath the city of Liverpool. This was the first tunnel in the world to be dug beneath a major metropolis. At last, the Liverpool-Manchester line was nearing completion with its biggest hurdles overcome. Now only the question of motive power remained.

By September, the *Rocket* was ready and shipped to Rainhill for the competition. The event took on the look and feel of a race meet. Each of the entrants was given a color and would have to complete 60 miles up and down the track. Engineers and deputations from other countries were present to observe, including at least two from prospective American lines. For George Stephenson, this was a debate which was perfectly suited to his character. He would not have to be concerned here with marshaling his words, overcoming the hindrance of his thick, regional accent or his origins from an impoverished mining family. At Rainhill, he would be proved right based solely on the product of his genius.

In the end, there was little contest. The *Rocket* proved fast and reliable and was the only engine to complete all the required tests successfully and without breakdowns. It completed twice the distance without mechanical failures than its nearest rival. The news of its success was carried far from the United Kingdom, prompting an explosion of railway creation in the United States on the basis of first-hand accounts and newspaper reports of the trials. Finally, Stephenson had been proven correct. Locomotives could work, and his were by far the best. The *Rocket* remains the invention for which Stephenson is most well remembered. Its development helped springboard the popularity of locomotive steam engines without which the face of the United Kingdom would have looked very different over the course of the next century.

The Rainhill trials resulted in orders of four *Rocket*-type locomotives from the Stephenson works. Following this success, with the argument over locomotion compared to static engines finally won, Stephenson now had to prepare for the opening of the line which would be his showcase. The grand unveiling of the Liverpool-Manchester railway was scheduled for September 15, 1830. Stephenson was 49 years old at the time.

Stephenson would drive the *Northumbria*, the successor to the *Rocket*, at the head of a procession of locomotives entrusted to family members, such as his son and brother (both named Robert), and his staff. The opening would be attended by the elite of British society, including the prime minister and duke of Wellington, Arthur Wellesley. Thousands gathered in both Liverpool and Manchester to see the procession. There was an incident en route in which one member of Parliament, William Huskisson, was run over by the *Rocket* and killed. This was an unfortunate accident, but it seems not to have detracted from Stephenson's triumph overall.

Unlike the Stockton-Darlington line, this was what would be described today as a major news story, and it made George Stephenson a worldwide celebrity. There was an insatiable public appetite for commemorations of the event, and a glut of items reached the market including Liverpool-Manchester handkerchiefs, tea towels, medals, tea trays, tumblers, snuff boxes, mugs, and many other items.

Over the next ten years, two manias would grip the country. The first was railway mania, and it would seize public and business alike. The second was George Stephenson as railway builder, which seemed to overcome those men who wished to build railways. Stephenson had more work than he could handle and railways were in demand in every part of the United Kingdom. As well as this, Stephenson was advising and acting as a consultant for visiting engineers from across the world. Americans, in particular, would visit Newcastle to see the Stephenson locomotive works.

Chapter Nine

The Railway Mania in Stephenson's Last Years

"Take him for all in all, we shall not look upon his like again. Nay, we cannot, for in his sphere of invention and discovery, there cannot again be a beginning."

—Obituary to George Stephenson

The Liverpool-Manchester railway was extremely profitable, and it made Stephenson, and his pupils, the popular choice for engineer by any railway board. Stephenson worked on the Leicester-Swannington railway next, which was completed in 1833. He missed out on some important projects at the same time, due to his inflexibility in his approach. When asked to survey a Lancaster-Carlisle line, he insisted that the line had to circle for miles out of its way to avoid the hills of the Lake District. But modern locomotives possessed the power to climb steeper hills than those that had first plied the Liverpool-Manchester line. He lost the commission to his former protege, Joseph Locke, who ran the line directly over the hills. Stephenson missed out on the Grand Junction (the junction of Liverpool and Birmingham lines) due to his haphazard method of surveying. Again, it was Locke who was awarded the job of engineer. The same reason cost Stephenson the London-Brighton line.

But these were drops in the ocean amongst other important lines which Stephenson built and no more than minor irritations. On October 11, 1838, the Sheffield and Rotherham Railway was opened. The York and North Midland Railway opened on May 29, 1839, the Birmingham and Derby Junction Railway on August 12, 1839, and the Manchester and Leeds Railway was completed in 1840 as was the North Midland Railway. All had George Stephenson as the chief engineer. The workload he accepted can be seen by the closeness of the completion dates. All of these lines must have been under construction at the same time and probably were surveyed close to simultaneously as well. As noted, there were other projects that he failed to win which would also have been under construction in this period if Stephenson had his way.

It is understandable that by the 1840s, Stephenson was talking in his letters about retirement. He bought a house overlooking the town of Chesterfield, Tapton House. He also opened a coal mine and lime works in the area after noticing a rich coal seam while excavating for the Midlands railway. Stephenson didn't go into retirement proper until around 1844 and had two last battles to fight. Both came to him from the man who would grow to eclipse him in the eyes of history as one of Britain's greatest engineers, Isambard Kingdom Brunel.

The first was an argument over railway gauges. Brunel was employing a broad gauge for his Great Western

Railway, with seven feet between the rails. He argued that this allowed for wagons sitting between their wheels instead of on top, which gave more stability and allowed for higher speeds. Stephenson, of course, favored his own approach, 4 feet, 8.5 inches. Neither man would admit to anything but his own idea being the best. Brunel could point to record-setting speeds on the Great Western Railway, thanks to his broad gauge. Stephenson argued that no locomotive needed to travel faster than 40 miles an hour (a sign of changing times after being forced to keep quiet about going faster than ten miles an hour just a decade earlier).

A royal commission was set up in August 1845 to investigate the problem and decide which should be used. Unsurprisingly, the man who had heralded in the railway age, and who had a near monopoly on locomotive manufacture, won the day. Stephenson's standard gauge was decided to be the one which all new lines in the United Kingdom would employ. Brunel and the Great Western Railway were left with a white elephant which would not survive Brunel's death. The GWR would eventually tear up their broad-gauge tracks in favor of the standard. More interestingly, this argument appears to mirror the row over the miner's safety lamp. This time, George Stephenson won against the upper class, well-educated Brunel. Stephenson doubtlessly derived a great deal of satisfaction that—for once—he was the establishment.

The two would clash again over Brunel's experimental "atmospheric railway" which he proposed to run from

Newcastle to Berwick and which used a vacuum to pull the train along. Stephenson was commissioned to survey a more traditional railway route in the same place, and again he proved the more successful. The traditional railway would be constructed over the new design being championed by Brunel.

By the end of Stephenson's life, the man who had almost single-handedly invented the railway industry had come to represent the old order while a new generation was emerging to challenge his way of thinking and suggest new ideas.

By 1845, Stephenson was entirely occupied with his gardens at Tapton House and his ambition to grow a straight cucumber. His second wife, Elizabeth, died in 1845, and Stephenson remarried in 1848 to a much younger woman, Ellen. George Stephenson would not be allowed to enjoy his retirement for long, and he died of a severe attack of pleurisy on August 12, 1848. He was 67 years old. Stephenson was buried at Holy Trinity Church in Chesterfield beneath a stone slab to which was later added his name and a memorial window by his son, Robert.

Conclusion

The British Empire achieved its zenith in the late nineteenth century, and it could be argued that this would simply not have been possible had it not been for George Stephenson. Stephenson's ambitions for the locomotive steam engine started the craze for steam-powered public railways in Britain. The railways led to an explosion of growth for the British economy and made British industry and commerce pre-eminent. The technology which George Stephenson pioneered laid the foundation for the engines which the next generation of engineers would use to power ships carrying British goods across the world.

Had it not been for Stephenson's genius at engineering and his unshakeable confidence in that ability, as well as his determination, the mines and factories that powered the British economy would have labored on with human and horsepower for many years to come. The country would have remained a place of isolated communities, days or even weeks of travel apart, and downtrodden workers under the control of wealthy industrialists who were effectively feudal barons. Steam power cut down on manual labor, reduced the price of goods, and made the country much smaller.

Stephenson also showed the world that no socio-economic class system was unbreakable. He emerged from the lowest point of the British class hierarchy, the impoverished northeastern pitman. Hardly any groups had fewer prospects. And yet, he rose from those beginnings to dominate society. Without money behind him except what he could earn for himself, with no education but what he could teach himself, he shook off his humble origins to become a wealthy landowner and a man known and respected throughout the world.

The creation of the Liverpool-Manchester line set in motion a mania for railways that is hard for a modern reader to comprehend. For anyone living in Britain today, railways are part of the landscape in every community, large or small. It is part of the British transport infrastructure and as such goes largely unnoticed. But in 1830, it did not exist. It was brought into being by George Stephenson. It ushered in the beginnings of the modern age.

George Stephenson and the *Rocket* have become immortal as a result. Many millions of Britons know what both Stephenson and his most famous locomotive look like because for many years both appeared on the five-pound note. So, in the end, the penniless, illiterate lad from the Tyneside pits achieved immortality.

Printed in Great Britain
by Amazon